Crochet for Beginners

The most complete Step By Step Guide to quick and easy crochet learning with illustrations including amazing crochet pattern Ideas

EMILY MAKER

© **Copyright 2021 by CAMELIA ROMERO- All rights reserved.**

This document is geared towards providing exact and reliable information in regards to the topic and issue covered. The publication is sold with the idea that the publisher is not required to render accounting, officially permitted, or otherwise, qualified services. If advice is necessary, legal or professional, a practiced individual in the profession should be ordered.

- From a Declaration of Principles which was accepted and approved equally by a Committee of the American Bar Association and a Committee of Publishers and Associations.

In no way is it legal to reproduce, duplicate, or transmit any part of this document in either electronic means or in printed format. Recording of this publication is strictly prohibited and any storage of this document is not allowed unless with written permission from the publisher. All rights reserved.

The information provided herein is stated to be truthful and consistent, in that any liability, in terms of inattention or otherwise, by any usage or abuse of any policies, processes, or directions contained within is the solitary and utter responsibility of the recipient reader. Under no circumstances will any legal responsibility or blame be held against the publisher for any reparation, damages, or monetary loss due to the information herein, either directly or indirectly.

Respective authors own all copyrights not held by the publisher.

The information herein is offered for informational purposes solely, and is universal as so. The presentation of the information is without contract or any type of guarantee assurance.

The trademarks that are used are without any consent, and the publication of the trademark is without permission or backing by the trademark owner. All trademarks and brands within this book are for clarifying purposes only and are the owned by the owners themselves, not affiliated with this document.

Contents

Introduction 7

Chapter 1: Basics of Crochet 9

1.1 What Is Crochet? 9

1.2 Essential Crochet Tools Every Beginner Should Have .. 9

1.3 Common Crochet Terms 15

1.4 How To Hold The Crochet Hook? 16

1.5 How To Crochet With One Needle? 18

Chapter 2: How To Read A Crochet Pattern? 19

2.1 Reading Crochet Pattern 21

2.2 Symbols 22

2.3 Levels Of Skill 22

2.4 Details Of The Pattern 23

2.5 Abbreviations 23

2.6 Look At The Stitches And Abbreviations Used In The Pattern 26

2.7 Tips And Tricks For Reading A Crochet Pattern 26

2.8 How To Understand A Crochet Pattern In Another Language? 28

Chapter 3: Basic Crochet Methods 30

3.1 Single Crochet Stich 30

3.2 Double Crochet Stich 35

3.3 Chain Stich 45

3.4 Slip Stitch 49

3.5 Half Double Crochet 52

4

Chapter 4: Quick And Easy Beginner Crochet Patterns 57

4.1 Crochet Scarf 57

4.2 A Crochet Beanie 60

4.3 Crochet Kitty 64

4.4 Baby Lamb Farm Animal Crochet Pattern 67

4.5 Baby Blanket Crochet Pattern 72

4.6 Crochet Mitten Pattern 76

4.7 Crochet Pattern For Autumn Sweater 83

Chapter 5: What Every Beginner Crocheter Should Know? 88

5.1 With A Pattern Repetition, How Do You Change Your Base Chain? 88

5.2 Which Chain Should You Start With? 89

5.3 The Question Of How Much Yarn To Purchase? 89

5.4 How To Alter The Colors? 90

5.5 How To Secure The Ends And Weave Them In? 91

5.6 What Is The Best Way To Block A Blanket? 91

5.7 How Do You Frog? 92

Chapter 6: 10 Common Mistakes and How to Prevent Them? 93

6.1 Not Being Able To Distinguish Between Chains 93

6.2 Maintaining Order In Your Project 94

6.3 Not Understanding Gauge 95

6.4 Weaving In The Ends Correctly 97

6.5 Difficulty In Joining Rounds Correctly 97

6.6 Not Knowing How To Read Crochet Patterns Correctly 99

6.7 Not Understanding The Pattern In Its Entirety..........*100*
6.8 Not Using Stich Markers For Marking Start Of Round *101*
6.9 Not Grasping The Concept Of Tension *101*
6.10 Using The Wrong Hook Size And Yarn For The Task *102*

Conclusion **103**

Introduction

The art of crochet we practice today was developed during the 16th century. Crochet is derived from the French word croc or croche, which means hook.

Crochet is a textile created from a single thread which is looped over and over again with the use of a hook. It's looped such that pulling the thread through the preceding stitch creates a new stitch. While there are many forms of handwork that can be traced back in time, such as knitting, embroidery, and weaving, it is unclear when and where crochet began. Crochet items are mostly produced for the enjoyment of creating attractive patterned motifs. Crocheting was recognized as the major source of income among people living in remote villages throughout the early eras of imperialism, where the craft was practiced in the western portion of Europe. Wearing a crocheted item is seen as a statement of riches and authority by most royals. Crocheting is popular these days for many individuals. It has evolved into a skill for making excellent crochet items and patterns.

A hook is the instrument used to crochet; it was once made of wood, but now aluminium or steel hooks are available in a variety of sizes. Animal bones and horns were occasionally used as hooks. Along with hook the other basic thing required for crocheting is yarn. A person can purchase a variety of threads and yarns to produce a crochet product. Depending on the sort of design or pattern he wants to make, he can select from a variety of textures and colors. In today's market, there are some fundamental sorts of yarns.

Like with any craft, the finer you are at basic abilities, the easier it is to produce things. It's vital for a beginner to grasp the various types of materials, and their impact the final item, and the language used by other crafters to explain the process.

You won't achieve the results you desire if you don't recognize the difference in hook sizes, can't identify worsted yarn from fingering yarn and don't swatch to check the tension before beginning a new project. Crocheting is a wonderful art and like any new skill, you must first understand what you're doing in order to achieve the finest results.

Chapter 1: Basics of Crochet

1.1 What Is Crochet?

Crochet is a fabric-making technique that involves interlocking threads, yarn or strands of many other materials with a crochet hook. Crocheting differs from knitting in a few ways. Crochet finishes stitches before moving on to the next, whereas knitting leaves multiple stitches open at once. The surface expands in a circular, spiral, or to and fro motion. The most popular themes are geometrical and floral.

1.2 Essential Crochet Tools Every Beginner Should Have

Crocheting is a pleasant, useful, and cost-effective pastime. Crocheting, on the other hand, is a handcraft that necessitates the use of certain hand-held equipment.

The hook and yarn are the two most important crochet tools that you can't live without. You can't crochet anything without them. There are several more tools that are beneficial and should be included in your toolkit.

Hook

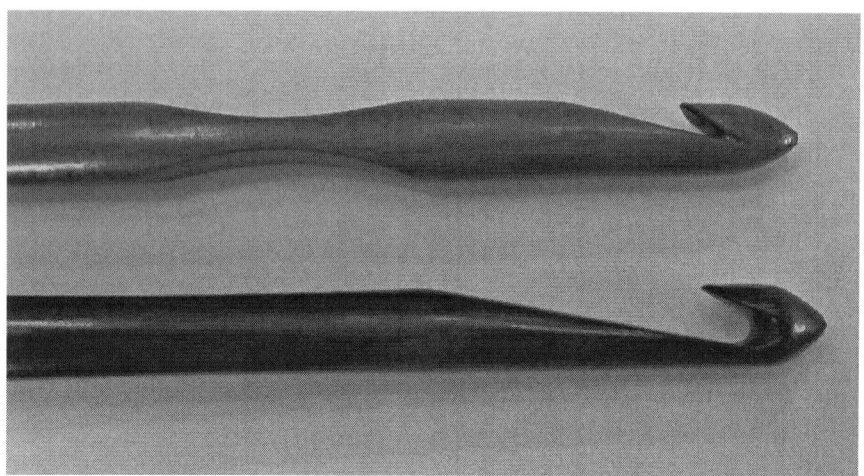

A single hook is used to crochet. Crocheting hooks are available in a variety of lengths and sizes, depending on the yarn you're using. Yarns are indicated with recommendations for the hook size that would work best with them.

Crocheting hooks are affordable, but you don't need to buy one of each size hook in the store if you're a novice. Start with a medium-sized hook, or get a variety pack that contains the most common sizes.

Crocheting hooks are available in a variety of styles, including ones with ergonomic or cushioned handles, as well as some that are hand-carved from wood. These are lovely additions, and you may enjoy working with them, but nothing complicated is required.

Yarn

Yarns are available in a wide range of materials, colours, textures, weights, and durability levels. They might be inexpensive or extremely costly, as well as anything in between. Silk, acrylic, cotton, and animal wool (goat, sheep, alpaca, rabbit...) yarns, as well as mixes, are all available. Cotton or cotton-linen mixes are more durable and can endure washing and heavy usage, but alpaca wool, soft sheep or other natural fibres feel nice on the skin but require a little more attention.

If you like colours, textures, and fabrics, choosing your yarn may be one of the most exciting elements of starting a project. The sort of yarn you choose should be chosen by the item's intended purpose—for example, while crocheting a washcloth, you'd use a tougher yarn than when you are crocheting a baby blanket.

If you're a novice, it's also a good idea to start with easy-to-work-with yarn: nothing too fine, fluffy, slippery, silky, or knobby. As your abilities improve, you may experiment with more delicate or textured fabrics. Beginners should start with lighter-colored yarns that are smooth in texture but not slippery.

Stich Markers

Locking stitch markers are particularly handy if you plan to put a partially finished item aside for a while and don't want any of the crochet stitches to come undone.

Yarn Snippers or Scissors

For cutting the yarn at the start and end of projects, you'll need a pair of scissors. Any pair in good functioning order would suffice, but for crocheting, a tiny pair with a sharp end for cutting is the most practical. These are also useful if you have any special yarn.

Darning Needle

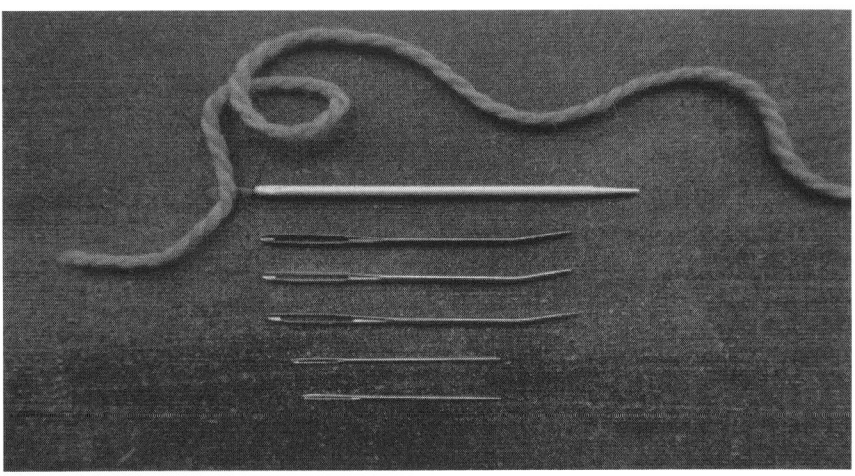

Darning needles or Tapestry needles are used to stitch in the yarn ends and to join the crocheted cloth together at the conclusion of a project.

Make sure you have both a blunt-tipped needle and a sharp needle on hand. Sharp points make stitching in the ends simpler, while blunt tips make completing the seams easier. The needle size you require may also be determined by the thickness of the yarn. To thread a thick yarn, for example, you'll need a needle with a bigger eye.

Ruler or Tape Measure

When you're trying to produce an item of a specific size, a ruler or a tape measure is a useful tool to be in your crocheting kit. You may be able to depend on your sight for basic items like washcloths or scarves without needing to measure anything. Taking measurements, on the other hand, will help you to create a patched crochet quilt or anything that requires more accuracy.

1.3 Common Crochet Terms

Skein of yarn: It is the standard yarn configuration seen in most craft stores. You may pull a skein from either the middle or the side.

Hank of yarn: A hank of yarn is coiled into a big, loose circle before being firmly twisted together.

A ball of yarn: It is yarn that has been rolled into a ball. Although yarn is not usually purchased as a ball, many crocheters and knitters wrap a hank of yarn to a ball.

Fasten off: Making a knot at the completion of your project to keep it from unravelling is referred to as fastening off.

Gauge: Gauge relates to the tightness or looseness with which you crochet. It's the measurement of how big or little each stitch should be. Some crocheters work with a very tight gauge, while others work with a looser gauge. It's a matter of personal choice, but when you require a crochet product to be a specific size, it's critical that your gauge matches that of the pattern's creator. As a result, their gauge size may be included in the design for you to match.

Turning chain: The chain you construct at the end of a row is known as a turning chain. Before you flip the product over and start the next row, the pattern may indicate "chain 2."

Yarn over: Yarn over refers to wrapping the yarn around the hook. Yo is a common abbreviation.

1.4 How To Hold The Crochet Hook?

Crochet hooks are available in a variety of sizes, ranging from some fine steel hooks for exquisite doilies and lace to bigger hooks made of aluminium, plastic, or wood for Afghans, clothes, and household goods.

The most common hooks are roughly 6 inches in length and are labeled in alphabetical order from B (refers the smallest) to Q (refers the largest).

Since the crochet hook is perhaps the most crucial instrument you'll use while learning to crochet, it's critical to know what each portion does and how it works.

At first appearance, a crochet hook seems to be a straight piece with a hook attached to the end. When you look closely, though, you'll notice that each hook usually has five pieces. When learning how to crochet, it's crucial to understand what each element does.

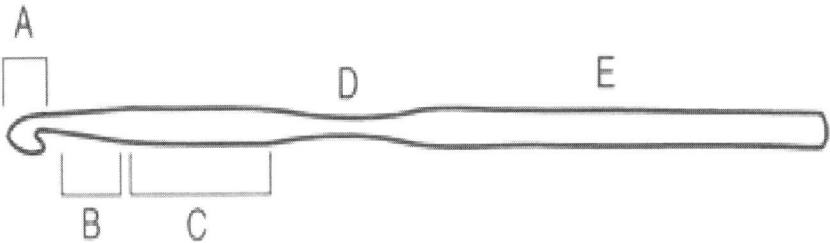

The first one is the hook tip (A), and is used to hook and drag the yarn through other loops (called stitches). The throat (B) is an area designed on the crochet hook that allows you to move the stitch up onto working area (C). The flattened portion of the thumb rest or finger hold (D) helps you grasp the hook comfortably, generally with the thumb and third finger. The handle (E), which sits beneath your 4th and 5th fingers offers balance for simple and smooth work, is the fifth and final component.

Every stitch must be made on the working region, not on the throat (B), which would cause the stitch to be excessively tight, or on the finger grip (D), which would cause the stitch to stretch.

The crochet hook can be held in a variety of ways. You'll have to experiment to discover the method that seems the most natural to you. Your hand will cramp up if it isn't comfortable, and the stitches will be uneven. Play around with several options until you discover one that seems most appropriate to you.

1.5 How To Crochet With One Needle?

Many people mix up the phrases "crochet" and "knit," believing they are interchangeable. While they are similar, there are a few significant distinctions. For one example, if you show a knitted item to a crochet buddy and ask them to create it, they might not be able to. K nit and Crochet patterns are quite different, and it is difficult to convert a knit pattern to a crochet pattern. Knitting necessitates the use of two knitting needles and differs from crochet in the way yarn is interlocked. Knitting involves transferring the complete item through one knitting needle to the next.

Crochet uses only one hook, and instead of moving the object from one needle to another, the final product is left on the fabric itself. Another significant distinction is the way knit and crochet feel. A finished knitting swatch will differ from a finished crochet swatch in appearance and feel. Knitting is relatively soft than crocheting. Crochet consists of knots piled adjacent to and on top of each other.

While there is a dispute over which is better, for beginners, crocheting is recommended over knitting. There's a good reason for this: if you make a mistake with crochet, it's far easier to unravel the product and correct it. It's far more difficult to repair errors while knitting.

Chapter 2: How To Read A Crochet Pattern?

Knowing how to interpret crochet patterns will introduce you to a whole new world of crochet. You'll be able to advance your skills beyond the fundamentals and tackle increasingly difficult tasks.

Nothing is more aggravating than spending time and money on the perfect crochet design only to discover it is written incorrectly or in a style you are unfamiliar with. It is believed that we've all been there at some point in our lives. First and foremost, let's be clear. A written pattern is nothing more than a way for a designer to convey a set of instructions to a reader. You will comprehend this if you study it one section at a time, learning one bit at a time. Consider it a form of decoding.

Learning the writing style, particularly the crochet symbols and abbreviations is key to learning how to read crochet patterns. It's not essential to remember all of the symbols and abbreviations at once; instead, consult the lists as you come across these words in your crochet designs.

When reading crochet designs, keep the following in mind:

- Crochet designs can be done in rows or rounds. Depending on the design, you'll be working in rows, rounds, or a combination of the both.

- Most crochet designs are categorized into beginner, easy, intermediate, and expert levels of complexity. Select the degree of difficulty that best suits your crochet skills. Avoid the frustration of attempting to work with a complicated crochet design. You would be able to effectively handle more challenging designs as you get more crochet skill.

- It's critical to keep track of the stitches as you work to ensure that each row or round has the number of stitches specified in the pattern.

- Always keep an eye on your gauge. While it may not be as essential if you are doing a project for that you have an endless supply of yarn or thread and don't care what size it ends out to be, if you are making a project that has to be the size stated in the pattern, you will be putting yourself up for disappointment. Crochet a 4 inch by 4 inch sample with in stitch pattern used for the crochet instructions to verify your gauge. Try a smaller hook if your gauge is bigger than the gauge specified in the design. Use a bigger hook if your gauge is smaller.

Reading crochet designs takes practice, so don't give up if you don't comprehend all of patterns you want to crochet right away. The more you practice, the more it becomes second nature. You'll be able to understand any crochet pattern you choose in no time.

2.1 Reading Crochet Pattern

A pattern written in conventional crochet abbreviations appears to most beginners to be a foreign language. To make things easier, here are written two rows of the single pattern in conventional crochet abbreviations first, then in regular English. As you can see, drafting a pattern in conventional crochet abbreviations requires a lot less space and makes it easier to concentrate on the instructions.

- Row 1 is written as follows in standard crochet abbreviations:
- Row 1: Ch 15, (sc) in 2nd ch from hook and in every ch across, flip with size H hook.
- (14 sc)
- Row 1 now appears as follows in Standard English:
- Row 1: Chain 15 stitches with a size H crochet hook, single crochet in second chain stitch from hook and for every chain stitch across, flip. (At the conclusion of this row, there are now 14 single crochets.)
- After you've finished row 1, move on to row 2. It looks like this when written in conventional crochet abbreviations:
- Row 2; Ch 1, 2 sc in the first sc, sc in every rem sc across to the last sc, 2 sc in the last sc, flip. Row 3: Ch 1, 2 sc in the

first sc, sc in every rem sc across to the last sc, 2 sc in the last sc, flip. (16 sc)

Row 2 is written in normal English as follows:

- Row 2; Chain 1, work two single crochets in first single crochet of the row 1, stitch a single crochet for each leftover single crochet of row 1 other than the last single crochet, turn. (For a total of 2 increased stitches, increase 1 stitch in first single crochet in this specific row and 1 stitch in last single crochet of this row.) At the conclusion of this row, there are total 16 single crochets.)

2.2 Symbols

Symbols are used in crochet designs to indicate repeated text, specific directions, and clarifying information.

( ) Work instructions in italic text within parenthesis in location instructed; used to show collective stitch groups performed as one operation in the same area; utilized for extra or clarifying information.

2.3 Levels Of Skill

The skill level is usually shown in the first part of a design. Consider where you are in the crocheting experience and whether you are prepared to tackle a new project. A Basic or Beginner level pattern is a wonderful place to start practicing your pattern reading abilities because the instructions are simpler.

2.4 Details Of The Pattern

The type of yarn the artist used in the project, as well as quantity, notions (including hook size), final piece measurements, and gauge, will all be given in the pattern. Before the real instructions, stitches and unique stitch combinations will be provided. The designer will frequently believe you are familiar with the simplest stitches and will include instructions for the less popular stitches as well as unique stitch combinations.

2.5 Abbreviations

Crochet abbreviations are used in written patterns. Knowing how to interpret a crochet pattern requires an understanding of crochet abbreviations. A collection of crochet abbreviations can be found below.

CROCHET ABBREVIATIONS

[ ]	work instructions within brackets as many times as directed	FPtr	front post treble crochet
( )	work instructions within parentheses as many times as directed	g	gram
*	repeat the instructions following the single asterisk as directed	hdc	half double crochet
* *	repeat instructions between asterisks as many times as directed or repeat from a given set of instructions	inc	increase/increases/increasing
"	inch(es)	lp(s)	loops
alt	alternate	m	meter(s)
approx	approximately	MC	main color
beg	begin/beginning	mm	millimeter(s)
bet	between	oz	ounce(s)
BL	back loop(s)	p	picot
bo	bobble	pat(s) or patt	pattern(s)
BP	back post	pc	popcorn
BPdc	back post double crochet	pm	place marker
BPsc	back post single crochet	prev	previous
BPtr	back post treble crochet	rem	remain/remaining

CA	color A	rep	repeat(s)
CB	color B	rnd(s)	round(s)
CC	contrasting color	RS	right side
ch	chain stitch	sc	single crochet
ch-	refers to chain or space previously made (e.g., ch-1 space)	sc2tog	single crochet 2 stitches together
ch-sp	chain space	sk	skip
CL	cluster	Sl st	slip stitch
cm	centimeter(s)	sp(s)	space(s)
cont	continue	st(s)	stitch(es)
dc	double crochet	tch or t-ch	turning chain
dc2tog	double crochet 2 stitches together	tbl	through back loop
dec	decrease/decreases/decreasing	tog	together
dtr	double treble	tr	treble crochet
FL	front loop(s)	trtr	triple treble crochet
foll	follow/follows/following	WS	wrong side
FP	front post	yd(s)	yard(s)
FPdc	front post double crochet	yo	yarn over
FPsc	front post single crochet	yoh	yarn over hook

2.6 Look At The Stitches And Abbreviations Used In The Pattern

Most designs contain a list of stitches and their abbreviations used by the designer. Reading patterns, like always said, is like decoding a hidden code; this is your secret. If there is a stitch that you are unfamiliar with and there isn't an explanation for it, perform a quick search to see if you can locate a lesson before beginning the design. If you need to locate the instructions later, bookmark or write them down.

2.7 Tips And Tricks For Reading A Crochet Pattern

- As you proceed, make notes about the pattern. A pattern is generally photocopied fo convenience. That way, you will have a rough and ready version to throw in your crochet bag and write on.
- As you finish each row cross it off from your list
- Make some "translate" notes of your own. If the pattern reads R9-13: sc around, for example, you will mark down the number "5" to indicate that you need to create five rows of single stich of crochet. Then, when you finish each row, you will cross it off the list.
- Mark the start of each round with a scrap of yarn.

- After each round, keep a tally. Especially if the round is challenging

- Recognize the pattern. Frequently, a row will include a part that is just repeated, with something new to begin and something new to conclude. Read and comprehend what you will be doing in the row. Pause. Then go to the first section. Then there are all of your repetitions. Then return to the pattern for the final portion.

- It's fine to take your time and crochet just few stitches before double-checking your work. When you are completing difficult rows, then you should take your time and double-check that you comprehend everything right. This is very normal behavior.

- If you follow the directions and something doesn't work out, don't toss your work down and scream that the instruction has to be incorrect. You're wrong 9 times out of 10. But it's all right. Read the instructions again. Have you skipped a step? Even the most seasoned crocheter makes mistakes from time to time. Consider the question, "What is the overarching goal of this row?" This can sometimes assist in determining the source of the problem.

- If you just can't seem to understand it. You can read a crochet pattern, however the pattern is actually incorrect. If you ended up on the correct stitch but the stitch count is incorrect, it's possible that simply the count is incorrect. It's possible that the guidelines are inaccurate if things are awry and you can't figure it out. If that's the case, you have a few choices:

- Look at the previous or next row and see if you can find any "clues" as to what should happen in the issue row. You can sometimes use your investigative skills to find out what is lacking or incorrect in the printed directions.

2.8 How To Understand A Crochet Pattern In Another Language?

Decoding a pattern in a different language can be difficult, and it is common that even following the suggestions provided, you can't always get it right. But it's worth a shot, and here are some recommendations:

- You can use Translator to translate the entire web page if it's on an internet site. You can go over it again and see how much you comprehend. The words will occasionally be unusual and not expressed in the way you're used to, but you'll usually understand the essence of the pattern.

- Following that, pay great heed to the stitch counts that have been supplied. Amigurumi and other round-worked objects usually increase by 6 stitches evenly distributed on each round. As a result, you can usually tell which rows have risen and which rows have even work.

- You should examine the images to see if they reveal anything.

- Watch a video if one is available to see whether you can comprehend it that way mute the volume since listening to a foreign language that you don't understand makes it difficult for you to focus on what you are watching.

- If you still can't figure it out, then take a step back and consider what it is about that pattern that fascinates you. Concentrate on identifying just that one piece before incorporating it into a comparable pattern written in English. Frequently, it's a colour scheme or a specific stitch that draws your attention. You can utilize the alien design as a stepping stone to something else you are more familiar with. When looking for a pattern element, prefer to use the search box. For example, look up "flower granny square." Similar patterns may also be found and you can locate a similar by searching.

Chapter 3: Basic Crochet Methods

3.1 Single Crochet Stich

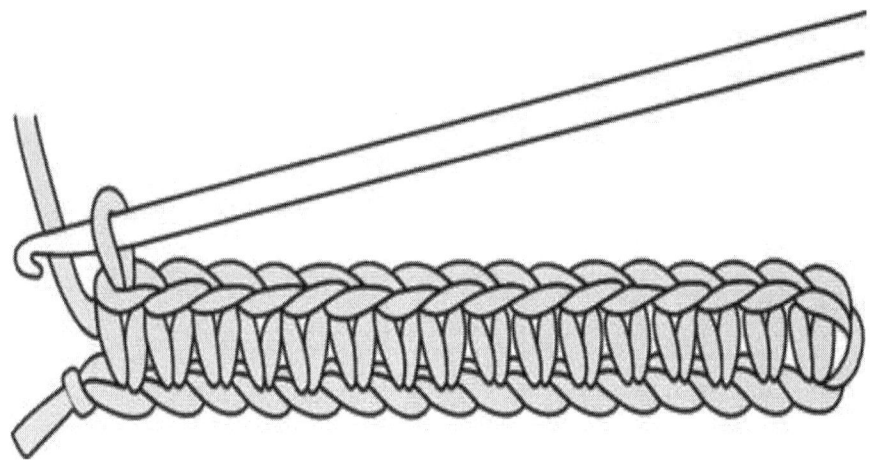

One of the basic crochet stitches is the single crochet stitch, which is also known as (sc). It's an easy-to-learn and fun-to-crochet stitch for beginners. Because single crochet is so popular, it's frequently the first method a beginner crocheter learns.

Single crochet is also quite flexible. For ribbing stitches, you can do single crochet in connected rounds, rows, spiral rounds, and different portions of the stitch. It may also be used to create borders, edges, and seams.

What is single crochet stich

Single Crochet Stitch is a crochet stitch that is used to make a single item. The single crochet pattern is a basic stitch that works well for a number of crochet items, including cushions, top-down beanies, and cozy sweaters. It's also commonly used in Amigurumi patterns and dolls too.

Abbreviation

Single crochet stich is abbreviated as (SC)

Symbol on the Chart

The single crochet is indicated by a "X" or a "+" in crochet charts.

Height

A single crochet stitch is shorter than that of a half-double crochet stitch and taller than a slip stitch.

Turning Chain

Form a turning chain of one chain stitch to create a new row of single crochet. (A turning chain is a series of chain stitches made at the start of a row to raise the yarn up to the proper height for the following stitch.)

Because the ch-1 will not count as a stitch, the first stitch of the next row will be inserted into the final stitch of previous row.

Fabric made from single crochet

A thick, solid crocheted fabric without any gaps or holes can be made with rows of simple single crochet.

Skill level: Basic

Materials Required: Yarn, A crochet hook

Step-by-step instructions of single crochet for right-handed beginners

- To secure the yarn to the hook, tie a slip knot.
- Repeat until you have linked 9 together then rotate the work so that you can start working the opposite way.
- Hook into the second chain from the hook.
- Yarn over (YO)
- Pull the yarn through the loop again; you should now have two loops on the hook.
- Yarn over (YO)
- A single crochet stitch has been finished by pulling yarn back across both loops on hook.
- Insert hook into next chain and continue steps 3–7 until row is complete (always insert the hook to a next chain when a single crochet is finished)
- To make a second row, chain 1 and then insert hook through both loops in second chain.
- Steps 3–7 should be repeated across the row till you reach the end.

- Remember to chain 1 at the finish of each row and flip your work before beginning a new row of single crochets if you want to make extra rows.

Step-by-step instructions of single crochet for left-handed beginners

- Make a chain to serve as a foundation. Chain 13 stitches for a 12 stitch practice swatch. Take note of the chain's front.

- Take a peek at the rear now. Take note of the distinction. You should be able to tell the front of a chain apart.

- The front of the chain should be towards you. In the second chain from off the hook, insert the hook. In both the front and rear loops, the hook should be placed under the upper section of the chain.

- Yarn over in the same way as you would for a chain stitch.

- Pull the hook through into the chain, catching the yarn in the process. To prevent the yarn from falling off the hook, keep the hook either pointing downward or facing you while you work. On the hook, there will be two loops.

- Yarn over the loops on the hook and pull the yard and hook through to the loops.

- You should now have one loop on the hook after completing one single crochet stitch.

- Put the hook into next chain stitch and continue the instructions above to create the next stitch.

- Carry on along the row. In each chain stitch, make a single crochet.

- Make a count of your stitches. Because the skipped initial chain stitch functioned as a turning chain, you began with 13 chain stitches and ended up with 12 single crochets.

- Make 1 chain stitch (the turning chain for the following row) after counting your stitches, and then flip your work over so the hook is now on the right side.

- Working extra rows differs from working the initial row. You'll now be knitting into the stitches of the row below, rather than a foundation chain. The single crochet stitch, on the other hand, will be created in the same way.

- The single crochet stitches' tops resemble chain stitches. On the top of the initial single crochet, slide the hook underneath the two strands that create the chain.

- Pull the hook back in after yarning over. On your hook, there should be two loops. Now yarn over and through the two loops with the hook. You've only made one crochet stitch so far.

- Make a single crochet for each single crochet from first row as you progress across the row.

- Make a count of your stitches. There should be 12 single crochets in total. The turning chain isn't included in the stitch count. Chain one more time and flip your work around so the hook is on the correct side. Rows should be worked in the same manner as the second row.

3.2 Double Crochet Stich

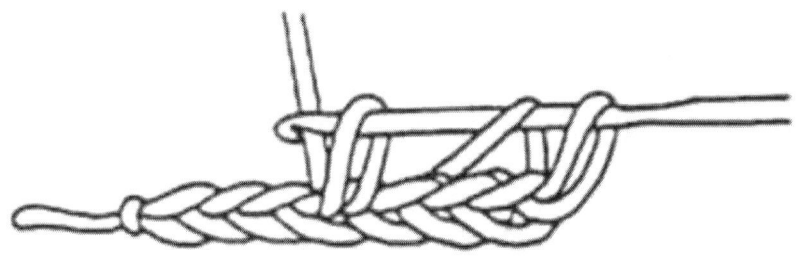

One of the most fundamental crochet stitches is double crochet. While you may crochet a variety of crafts without it, double crochet is a basic crochet stitch that virtually everyone learns as soon as they start crocheting.

If you wish to work most crochet designs, you'll need to learn how to double crochet. In rows and in the round, you can use the double crochet stitch by itself. It may also be used to make famous crochet stitch patterns like the popular v-stitch and traditional granny square.

Double crochet is fairly identical to single crochet, with the exception of a few additional steps.

Abbreviation

Double crochet stich is abbreviated as (DC)

Symbol on the Chart

In crochet charts, a single crochet is represented as a long "T" form with a diagonal cross.

Height

A double crochet stitch is comparably a taller stitch than a single crochet stitch. It's higher than a half double crochet but shorter if compared to a treble crochet stitch. It stands nearly twice as tall as a single crochet.

Turning Chain

Form a turning chain of three chain stitches to begin a new row of double crochet. (A turning chain is a series of chain stitches made at the beginning of each row to raise the yarn to the proper height for the upcoming row of stitches.)

The ch-3 is frequently mistaken for a double crochet stitch. That is, ignore the first stitch and weave first double crochet to the second.

For double crochet turning chain, certain patterns will only require two chains. In certain designs, the turning chain isn't counted as a stitch. Check your pattern if you're ever in question.

Fabric made from double crochet

A solid crocheted cloth with an excellent drape may be made with rows of simple single crochet. It's ideal for knitting baby blankets, sweaters, scarves, and other things since it's not too thick or stiff.

When Should You Do Double Crochet

When you need a sturdy cloth that comes together quickly, use double crochet stitches. It's ideal for crafts that require solidity and flexibility, such as granny squares, Afghans, coasters, and other similar products.

Skill level: Basic

Materials Required: Yarn, A crochet hook

Step-by-step instructions of double crochet for right-handed beginners

- A turning chain under the hook is used to begin a row in most designs. It's generally counted as a stitch, and in double crochet, it's made up of three chain stitches that are roughly the same height as the double crochet stitch. You'll know better whether or not to count it based on your pattern.

- Wrap the yarn around your crochet hook with one loop on the hook.

- Place the crochet hook in the appropriate stitch or area. Skip the three chains adjacent to the hook and put the hook to the fourth chain if you're beginning with a foundation chain. Place the hook inside the second stitch, not at the bottom of the turning chain.

- Wrap the yarn and over crochet hook once more while your hook is in the stitch.

- Wrapping the yarn over is similar to wrapping the yarn over just before inserting the hook. The difference is that your hook now has more yarn on it, making it a somehow little more difficult to manage. You'll get the idea of it in no time.

- 3 loops on the hook after pulling or "drawing" last and yarn over through spot where you placed the hook.

- Yarn over your hook once again, this time drawing this through the two loops nearest to the hook's end—two loops on the hook.

- Yarn over the hook once more and bring it through the leftover loops here on hook, 1 double crochet stitch completed when 1 loop on the hook.

- The turning chain towards the right side of the double crochet stitch that has been created may be seen here.

- Rows of double crochet stitches and working rows is the greatest approach to practice the double crochet stitch.

- For each stitch in the row, repeat the instructions above: Yarn over (yo) and insert; yarn over (yo) and draw through the material; yarn over (yo) and draw within two loops; yarn over (yo) and draw through the final two loops; yarn over (yo) and draw through last two loops. As you stitch, you will notice that the stitch has a rhythm to it. In fact, the processes are so similar that wrapping the yarn over drawing through the loops becomes one action.

- Work into the head of the preceding row's turning chain at the end of a row, flip the work, and then chain 3 to start another row. The more you practice this stitch, the more it becomes second nature. You'll notice that your stitches are becoming more even and that they're working up faster.

Step-by-step instructions of double crochet for left-handed beginners

- Make a foundation chain in any length you choose.

- Yarn over (YO)

- Hook into the fourth chain from the hook. Moving from left to straight away from your hook, that's the fourth chain to the right.

- Yarn over (YO)

- Draw a loop across it. At the conclusion of this stage, you should have three loops on the hook.

- Yarn over and pull the hook over the first two of the three loops.

- Reverse the yarn and draw it through the two loops on the hook. You've just finished the first double crochet stich.

- Rep steps 4–7 for the next stitch. Yarn over and slide crochet hook over to the next stitch.

- Step 8 should be repeated across the row.

- Turn the job around. Chain 3 is used to spin the chain.

- Yarn across and into the next stitch using the hook.

How to work in a round with Double Crochet

It's just as simple to work with double crochet in the round as it is in the rows. Double crochet in a round can be done in two ways.

- In rounds that are linked

- In circular loops that never stop

Rounds that are joined together

How to execute double crochet in connected rounds is as follows: With a chain-3, begin a new round. A stitch counts as a chain. Continue until you reach the last stitch. Finish the round with the last stitch. Connect the last stitch of the circle to the top of the ch-3 using a slip stitch. This brings the round to a close.

Rounds that go on indefinitely or in a spiral

To work in spiral/continuous rounds, simply proceed to the first stitch of each round when you reach the end of the previous round. The rounds are joined using a slip stitch, and there is no flipping chain between rounds.

When working in a spiral or continuous rounds, use a stitch marker to indicate the beginning of each round. You won't lose your spot this way.

Increases and Decreases

How to make a double crochet increase in crochet

Double Crochet Increase is a technique for increasing the size of a crocheted item. It's quite simple to make a double crochet increase. It's sometimes written as "dc inc" in patterns. You can also see it written as "2 dc in next st," which means "two double crochet stitches in next stitch."

Simply create two DC in one stitch to make a DC increase. Your stitch count will rise by one stitch as a result of the increase.

Working three or four different double crochets into the very same stitch will result in even greater increases.

How to make a double crochet decrease in crochet

Crochet reductions combine two stitches into a single stitch. In double crochet, there are a number different ways to reduce. If you're working from a design, the pattern notes should specify which decreasing style to employ.

Double crochet decrease (traditional)

Double crochet is sometimes written as "dc dec" or "dc2tog" in designs. Here's how to put it together.

In the first stitch, insert the hook. Work a double crochet till two loops left on the hook in the last step. Those two loops should stay on the hook.

The hook should be inserted into the next stitch. Continue with next double crochet till you reach the last step. On the hook, there will be three loops left.

Then yarn over and pull the hook through all three loops. A typical double crochet reduction is now complete.

Double crochet decrease that isn't visible

If a standard double crochet decrease is too heavy for you, try this method for a less noticeable reduction.

When working with invisible reductions, it's important to reduce the stitch's base rather than its top.

To produce an undetectable double crochet decrease, follow these steps:

- Slip the hook into front loop of the very first stitch and yarn over.

- Instead of yarning over, put the hook to the front loop of next stitch right away.

- Then finish the double crochet by yarning over and drawing over the first two loops. Weave through to the next two loops after yarning over. Re-yarn the final two loops and draw through them.

Double Crochet Variations

You may start exploring the numerous variants of the fundamental double crochet stitch once you've learned it.

Working in Distinct Loops: To produce different textures, you may work double crochet either in the front or back loops.

Double Crochet Ribbing: You may make a flexible ribbing for sweater cuffs and hems by working rows of the double crochet with in back loop alone (DC BLO).

Herringbone Double Crochet: Using this stitch technique, you may create a solid fabric with a lovely zig-zag appearance.

Back Post/Front Post Double crochet: Crochet cables, elastic ribbing, and incredibly stitch patterns like the basket weave stitch and waffle stitch are all possible with double crochet.

Avoiding Common Errors While Doing Double Crochet Method

When learning double crochet for the first time, there are a few problems that beginners face.

Stitch count mistakes: You may have stitch count problems if your swatch appears to be expanding, decreasing, or skewing diagonally. You may not know it, but you're probably adding or deleting stitches that aren't supposed to be there.

Here are some suggestions for resolving the issue.

Don't create a dc into first stitch of the row since the turning chain also counts as a stitch. This results in an additional stitch. So, into the next stitch, create the first dc.

Make the final dc of the row to the top of the preceding row's turning chain. If you skip this last stitch, your stitch count will be reduced by one.

Count your stitches periodically to ensure you haven't acquired (or lost) any stitches inadvertently along the way.

Uneven edges: If the beginning of the row has unattractive gaps, consider chaining two rather than three stitches required for the turning chain. The use of a shorter turning chain can assist to reduce the look of holes at the start of rows.

3.3 Chain Stich

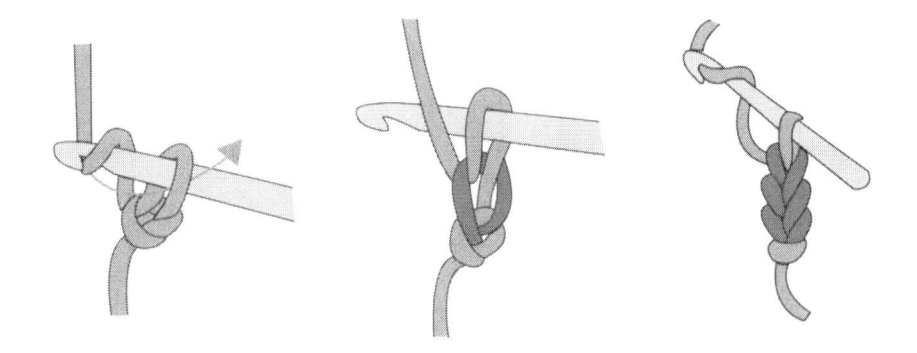

Crocheting is incomplete without chain stitches. Forming a sequence of chain stitches is generally the following stage in a project after making a slip knot. Chain stitches serve as the basis for the remainder of the project. They are one of a few basic stitches that each beginner should be familiar with.

Crochet designs frequently use chain stitches throughout the pattern, in addition to the foundation chain. Chain stitches are used to construct stitch patterns, create gaps between motifs, and shape cloth by combining them with other stitches. They may be used as laces for baby booties, ornamental thread for tying presents, and ornament hangers as simple chains.

It takes some work to keep your tension perfect for chain stitches, but it's a simple stitch to master.

Abbreviation

Chain stich is abbreviated as (ch)

Skill level: Basic

Equipment / Tools

Crochet hook in size according to yarn

Materials

Yarn

Step-by-step instructions of chain stich for right-handed beginners

- On your hook, tie a slip knot first. Grasp the knot with your left hand's thumb and middle fingers, using the slip knot made on the crochet hook. You should be facing the slip knot. The working yarn, the thread that comes from the ball, should run over your index finger, through your index and middle fingers, over your palm, and back to your ring and little finger. This may seem strange at first, but it will assist you in tensioning the yarn as you construct stitches and require additional yarn from the ball.

- Use a knife grip, pencil grip, or whichever grip seems most natural to you to hold the crochet hook in the right hand.

- Maintain the position of crochet hook pointing up to begin. When you make the chain stitches, keep your hold on the hook firm enough to retain control but flexible enough to let you to move freely.

- From back to front, loop the working yarn around the hook. Wrap the yarn around the crochet hook from the behind then over the top with your left hand, or move the hook with your right hand to achieve the same result. "Yarn over" or "Yarn round hook" or are terms used to describe this technique.

- To prepare for hooking the yarn, spin your crochet hook one quarter twist counterclockwise while looping it. It's fine to turn it a little more if necessary, but the aim is to keep each move as accurate and smooth as possible.

- Slide the hook downwards and then through the loop on the hook that is currently in place.

- If you reposition the hook towards its original position pointing upwards after bringing the yarn over, you will most likely find it simpler to complete the stitch.

- Making one chain stitch, you've just "chained one."

- Form a loop with the yarn over the hook to make another chain stitch. Rep as needed. Move your thumbs and index fingers up the freshly formed chain stitches as you crochet, remaining only one stitch or two away from hook loop. This will allow you to stitch with greater control and tension: not too tight, nor too slack.

- You'll develop a rhythm by spinning the crochet hook once you yarn over and then back as you pull through a loop as you work. The procedure is easier and faster when you have a rhythm.

Step-by-step instructions of chain stich for left-handed beginners

- Hold the hook in your left hand and the yarn in your right hand.
- Make a slipknot with the yarn and attach it to the crochet hook.
- Slip the slipknot onto the shaft of hook.
- Move the hook back under the yarn, then forward over it, beginning with the hook in the front of the yarn.
- As a result, the yarn has wrapped itself around the hook.
- Grab the yarn by turning the hook towards you while pulling the hook aside from the stitch to slightly open the loop.
- Slip the yarn through into the hook's loop, As a result, a new stitch is created.
- Continue in this manner until you have the appropriate number of chain stitches.

3.4 Slip Stitch

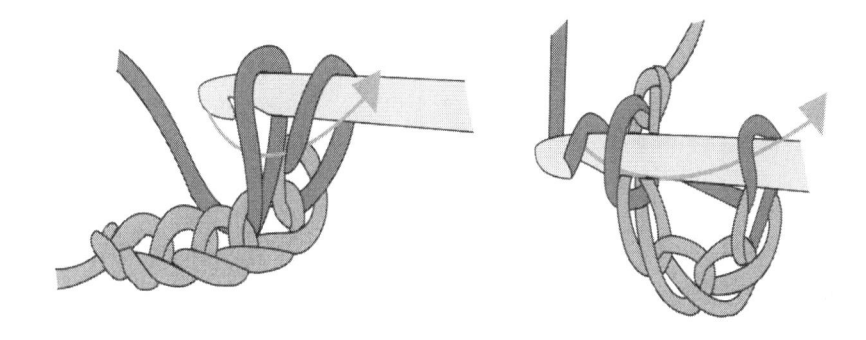

Slip stich is a simple crochet stitch that every beginner should know. It can even be used by knitters. Slip stitch may be used to connect parts, add ornamental features, and complete tasks with simple edging.

Because slip stitch is shorter than single crochet, it may be used in patterns as a means to create a smaller stitch. It's also a versatile stitch with several applications.

Slip stitch edging assist smooth the hem or sides of a garment, giving it a more completed appearance. It's usual to knit this in the same yarn as the rest of the project, but it's also enjoyable to add a pop of contrast.

Abbreviation

Slip stich is abbreviated as (sl st)

Height

The height of a slip stitch is quite low. It's used to connect stitches in a granny square that are knitted in rounds. It may also be used to go from one area of a row to another without leaving any visible stitches.

Equipment / Tools

Crochet hook in size according to yarn

Skill level: Basic

Materials: Yarn

Turning Chain

Make a turning chain of 1 to begin a new row of slip stitches. A stitch does not include the turning chain.

Step-by-step instructions of slip stich for right-handed beginners

- The hook should be inserted into the next stitch. Place the hook's tip beneath both loops just at top of the stitch.
- Slide a loop of yarn through into the stitch by bringing the yarn over through the hook from back to front.
- Pull the same loop through to the hook's loop as well. The slip stitch is now finished. There will only be one loop remaining on the hook at this point.
- You did an excellent job. You've just finished a slip stitch.

- You'll be able to draw the yarn over through loop on the hook and the stitch in one continuous motion once you've practiced.

Step-by-step instructions of slip stich for left-handed beginners

- Hold the hook in your left hand and the yarn in your right hand.
- In the front and rear loops, enter the hook into first chain, both under the top portion of the chain and the top part of the chain.
- Turn the yarn around and pull it through the turning chain and the loop on the hook. You've finished one slip stitch and created a ring.
- To crochet into the ring, place the hook in the centre of the ring and crochet as usual.

Edging using Slip Stitch

Slip stitch edging can be used to produce a smooth, completed border on various crafts. Make slip stitch into each stitch all along top and bottom edges, as well as equally along the sides, to form a simple slip stitch edging. What does "equally" indicate? For each and every row of single crochet, create one slip stitch, and for every row of double crochet, make two slip stitches. Also, while making a slip stitch edge, keep your tension slack because it's simple to make it too tight.

3.5 Half Double Crochet

The half double crochet pattern is a lovely crochet stitch that is both basic and flexible. When learning to crochet, a beginner should grasp one of the fundamental crochet stitches. These instructions will explain how to crochet the half double crochet stitch as well as some helpful hints for dealing with half double crochet. This stitch would be a good next step for beginners who already learned single crochet and double crochet.

In height, the half double crochet is halfway between a single crochet stich and a double crochet stich, but in half double crochet instead of working with two loops in the same time, you drag the yarn over three loops. It creates a cloth that is similar to one created using a single crochet stitch in terms of tightness.

It's a fundamental crochet stitch that's done in the same way as the other two. The reduced height and distinctive third loop are the result of a minor change.

Abbreviation

Half double crochet stich is abbreviated as (hdc)

Skill level: Basic

Materials Required: Yarn, A crochet hook

Step-by-step instructions of slip stich for right-handed beginners

- Complete (ch 15) 15 chain stitches. The foundation chain is built in this stage.
- Add 2 additional stitches to the chain. The turning chain is made up of these stitches.
- Insert the hook into the third chain from hook and yarn over the hook (yo).
- Wrap the yarn around the hook and carefully draw it into the chain stitch's centre, bringing the yarn that has been wrapped through the stitch.
- Draw the yarn through all three loops on the hook by wrapping it around the hook.
- Begin in the foundation chain's next chain. A whole line of half double crochet stitches is completed with this step.

- In each subsequent chain around the foundation chain, work 1 half double crochet stitch. At the conclusion of Row 1, you must have sixteen half double crochet stitches.

- Turn your work around. To begin Row 2, you must turn your work.

- Make a second chain (ch 2) put yarn over the entire hook (yo). The turning chain is made up of two stitches.

- Insert the hook in the next stitch after missing the very first stitch of the row right below the turning chain.

- By skipping the initial stitch, the number of stitches each row remains constant.

- In each of the following 14 half double crochet stitches, repeat the previous steps.

- From dragging the wrapped hook through to the middle of the chain stitch to bringing yarn through all three loops, repeat the steps.

- In the upper part chain of the preceding row's turning chain, work 1 half double crochet.

- In Row 2, you should have 16 half double crochet stitches.

Step-by-step instructions of slip stich for left-handed beginners

- Hold the hook in your left hand and the yarn in your right hand.

- This stitch is made in the same way as double crochet during the first few stages. This is why it's known as half-double crochet.

- Create a foundation chain comprising 14 stitches for a 12 stitch practice swatch. Yarn over and insert the hook into third chain from the hook while retaining the foundation chain front side facing you.

- Re-yarn the chain and slip the hook through that one. On your hook, you will now have three loops.

- Re-yarn the loops and pull the hook thru all the three. You should only have one loop here on hook at the end. You've just finished your first half-double crochet.

- Make one half-double crochet for each chain as you go down the row.

- Count your stitches when you've completed the row. In each row, there should be 12 half-double crochet stitches. Turn your work by chaining 2 with your turning chain.

- Put the hook into first stitch to make a half-double crochet. Place the hook beneath the "chain" on top of the stitch, just as you have done for the second row of single crochet. For each stitch across the row, work one half-double crochet. Work the last stitch into the preceding row's last half-double crochet.

- Count your stitches every time you sew. The row should consist of 12 stitches. To proceed, chain 2 and turn.

Chapter 4: Quick And Easy Beginner Crochet Patterns

4.1 Crochet Scarf

The simple scarf is a great project to start if you're new to crocheting. The moss stitch, a basic crochet pattern that combines chain stitches and single crochet and it is used to make this crochet scarf. The granite stitch or linen stitches are other names for the moss stitch. Making single crochet threads into gaps produced by chain stitches creates the moss stitch. It just takes a few rows to master this method, which results in a lovely contemplative pattern that is perfect for beginner and experienced crocheter. It's also simple enough for beginners, with no rising or decreasing required. This crochet scarf design is a great way to learn and practice this lovely stitch while also making a useful and pleasant item.

This is a fantastic beginner-friendly crocheting project to start with if you want to know how to crochet.

Finished Measurements / Sizing

4 inches in width

Approximately 50 inches in length

Crochet scarves exist in a variety of widths, so if yours is thinner or broader than the four, that's OK. No need to start over unless you like the width you've achieved, providing you bought enough yarn. If your scarf is significantly larger than 4 inches, the most pressing concern you'd have to worry about here is running out of yarn, as long as you're pleased with the width.

A crochet scarf's length is easily adjustable. Do you prefer a shorter scarf? Reduce the number of rows you crochet. Is it possible to get a longer scarf? Crochet a few extra rows as much as you have yarn.

Gauge

In Moss Stitch, 14 stitches and 15 rows equal 4 inches (10 cm).

Crochet seven to ten rows of pattern and measure the width of the item to determine your stitch gauge. Compare the initial measurement to the final measurement. If the scarf is turning out to be broader than the measurement provided, you may wish to start again with a smaller crochet hook. If it's getting too narrow, you might want to start a new with a bigger crochet hook.

Tools/ Equipment

Coil less safety pins or Stitch markers

6.5 mm crochet hook

Tapestry or yarn needle

Scissors

Materials

250 to 300-yard weight yarn

Pattern and Instructions

- Create a slip knot and then place it on the hook, leaving a six-inch tail of yarn; ch 15.

- In the very first ch from the hook, place a stitch marker. [Ch 1, skip in next ch, sc in the next ch] six times; flip. There will be 14 stitches total, with 7 sc stitches and 7 chain gaps (counting the space beside the indicated stitch).

- Row 2: [sc in next ch-1 sp, ch 1], [sc in next ch-1 sp, ch 1] Work sc into ch st where the marker was put six times, detaching the marker prior working the stitch. Turn.

- The remaining rows are identical to the previous row, with one tiny exception: at the conclusion of the row, work your final sc into the previous row's turning chain (tch).

- Rows 1–6: ch 1 (turning chain), [sc in next ch-1 sp, ch 1], work sc into tch.

- Repeat this row until the scarf is about 50 inches long or the desired length.

- Finish by fastening off, allowing enough yarn to weave in the ends. Using this end of yarn, thread the tapestry needle and weave it into the design so that it is hidden. Repeat with remaining stray threads you may have. That's all there is to it; now put the crochet scarf around the neck and enjoy it.

4.2 A Crochet Beanie

Do you need a last-minute present? Have you recently learnt to crochet? Is there a snowstorm on the way? Whatever your scenario, this super-easy crochet beanie will keep you warm. It's knit flat in a rectangle and afterwards seamed to make a hat, making it an extremely quick and thoughtless project to complete in under an hour.

Finished Measurements / Sizing

S: 18" x 14.5" (about 18" circumference, Un-stretched): for young teen

M: 20" x 14.5" (Unstretched circumference: approx. 20") for majority of women and men

L: 22" x 14.5" (about 22" Unstretched circumference) for heads with a larger circumference

Tools/ Equipment

Needle for tapestry

Crochet hook, size L (8 mm)

Safety pins or stitch markers

Small piece of cardboard/fur pom pom

Materials

Wool; 2 skeins (Mass: 5/ bulky – 124 yds, 4 oz.)

Gauge:

10 stitches = 4 inches

Just over 4 rows = 4 inches

Pattern and Instructions

- Rows of knitting are done back and forth on the hat. These rows will create the beanie's vertical ribs.
- The ch 3 only at start of each row is not counted as a stitch.

- To make this crochet hat design fit a toddler, start with less stitches and work considerably fewer stitches.

- After Row 1, double crochet stitches are only crocheted beneath the back loop of the preceding row's thread. Regardless of whether side of the crocheting is towards you, this is the loop furthest away from you.

- Ch 37 is the foundation row.

- Row 1: 1 dc in fourth ch from hook and that each ch to end of row; flip. Row 2: 1 dc in fourth ch from hook and that each ch to end of row; flip

- Row 2: Dcblo for each dc to the end of the row; turn

- Row 2 should be repeated 16 (18, 20) further times for a total of 18 (20, 22) rows.

- Fasten the ends together, separating the 24 inches tail. The size of the rectangle should be approximately.

- If you're right-handed, the tail of the final row will be on the bottom left once the WS is facing when you're determining the RS and WS of the fabric. If you're left-handed, the top left corner of your last row should have the WS facing you.

- Only work the seam between the chain stitches as well as the loop of every dc st closest to the seam to hide the connection.

- With the WS facing up, lay the rectangle horizontally. If desired, use safety pins or stitch markers to pin the seam.

- Tapestry needle with tail when fastening off threaded from the top of the dc st, work into the top of the corresponding ch. Then, starting from the bottom of the following ch, work into the base of the matching dc. Carry on in this manner from the peak of one dc to the peak of one ch, then from the bottom of one ch to the bottom of one dc. Rep till the seam is finished.

- Whip stitch across the top of the hat with tapestry needle and string of yarn left over from last seam, working 1 whip stitch into every row. Tighten the circle as much as possible, and then stitch up any leftover openings in the hat's top using a tapestry needle.

- Use a big pom pom machine or a 2.5" cardboard to make a pom pom.

- Put on your beautiful crochet hat and go to work creating one for someone you know.

4.3 Crochet Kitty

Crochet animals are so cute, and they're always a great thing when you're looking for an idea for the new creation. You can make crochet animals flat and two-dimensional, or you can make them in Amigurumi style (three-dimensional). They make perfect gifts for all ages, especially small children who can carry them everywhere and cuddle them to their hearts' content.

The prettiest tiny crochet cat design is the itty bitty crochet kitten. It's simple to create, an excellent project for beginners and would make a wonderful present for any cat lover.

Tools/ Equipment

Darning needle

Crochet hook, 3.25mm (larger cat)

Crochet hook, 2.75mm (smaller cat)

Material

Stuffing

DK cotton or Paint box yarns might also work well

Colors for the main body and a contrasting color for the face details

Pattern and Instructions

Body

- Mr. 6 sc, R1 (6)
- sc 2 in each row in R2 (12)
- [2 sc in next st, sc in next st] R3. recur around (18)
- [sc in the next 2 sts and 2 sc in the next st] R4. recur around (24)
- [sc in the next 3 sts and 2 sc in the next st] R5. recur around (30)
- [sc in the next 4 sts and 2 sc in the next st] R6. [sc in the next 4 sts, 2 sc in the next st] recur around (36)
- R7–8 sc all around (36)
- [sc in the next 4 sts and sc2tog] R9. [sc in the next 4 sts, sc2tog] recur around (30)

- Sc about R10–12 (30)
- [sc in the next 3 sts and sc2tog] R13. recur around (24)
- R14 - 17. sc all the way around (24)
- [sc in the next 2 sts and sc2tog] R18. recur around (18)
- R19. sc all the way around (18)
- Stuff. (*Now is the time to install safety eyes!)
- R20: Crochet across both sides, holding the top two edges together.
- dc in initial st, sc in each of the following 7 sts, dc in final st Bind off the ends and weave them in.

Tail

- Mr. 5 sc, R1 (5)
- R2: 2 sc in each round (10)
- R3. sc all the way around (10)
- R4. [sc2tog, sc3 in the next 3] repeat it (8)
- R5–6 sc all around (8)
- [sc2tog, sc in the next 2] R7. rephrase (6)
- Lightly stuff the tail's end.
- R8–15 sc all around (6)

- Bind off, leaving a tail to connect. There's no need to stuff it any farther!

- Change colours every 2–3 rounds if you'd like to add stripes.

- You may have a lot of fun giving your tiny kitten personality.

- First, sew the eyes in position, about 1 – 2 sts apart and 5 rows down to the end.

- You may also use safety eyes, but just be sure to put them on before finishing the last row. In pink, stitch the ear detailing and nose. Stitch any extra embellishments and add charming tiny whiskers in a gently contrasting hue. Attach the tail with a stitch. Give your kitten plenty of cuddles.

4.4 Baby Lamb Farm Animal Crochet Pattern

Lyla the Lamb is here to meet you! Lyla is a lively little lamb who is just poking its nose where it should not be. Lyla, on the other hand, has a way with people and can form friendships with anyone and everyone. She even gets along well with the sheepdogs.

Tools/ Equipment

Crochet hook, size E (3.50mm)

Yarn needle or tapestry

Marker for stitching

Materials

Worsted weight (4 ply) yarn in white, cream, and black

Eyes with a diameter of 9mm

Polyfil (or your filling or choice)

Pink embroidery floss (small amount for mouth)

Dimensions

3 in. (7.5 cm.) in length and 2 in. (5 cm.) in height

Pattern and instructions

The Pattern of the head (Starting in cream or black yarn)

- R1: Ch 2, 6 sc into 2nd ch from hook; R2: Ch 2, 6 sc into 2nd ch from hook; R3: Ch 2,

- R2: Rep 6 times *inc* (12 sts)

- Rep R3: *Sc 1, inc* 6 times (18 sts)
- Rep R4: *Sc 2, inc* 6 times (24 sts)
- Rep 6 times with R5: *Sc 3, inc* (30 sts)
- R6–8: Sc for all 30 sts (total of 3 rounds – 30 sts)
- Rep 6 times with R9: *sc 3, dec* (24 sts)
- We're going to make the curly fur now. The berry stitch will be used to create the fur curly (bs). Insert the hook to the stitch, yarn over, and pull through to form the berry stitch. Ch 4 now, working just with the front loop on the hook. Now yarn over and slide the hook through both loops. The berry stitch is finished.
- Basically, almost every stitch will be a bs from now on. Here the pattern is exactly as you will do it. Don't worry if you lose a bs here and there; it's a pretty forgiving stitch. Simply double-check your stitch count at the conclusion of each round.
- Rep 12 times with R10: *bs 1 and sc 1* (24 sts)
- R11: 12 reps of *Sc 1 and bs 1* (24 sts)
- 12 times R12: *Bs 1 and sc 1* (24 sts)
- R13: 12 reps of *Sc 1 and bs 1* (24 sts)
- 8 sts apart, insert eyes among R8 and 9. Count 8 stitches from the place where the first eye was placed and inserts the

second eye. Make a circle below the eyes with pink embroidery floss and stitch the nose. At the top, it should resemble a "Y" about 1.5 stitches wide.

- R14: 6 reps of *Sc 1, bs 1 and bs dec* (18 sts)
- Begin by producing a normal decrease by placing the hook through the first st, yarn over, and pulling through, then enter hook into next st, yarn over, and pulling through. Your hook now has three loops. Ch 4 with the loop nearest to the hook's tip, then yarn over and pull the hook across all loops. Your bs dec is finished.
- R15: 6 reps of *Bs 1, dec* (12 sts)
- Stop now and start stuffing.
- R16: 6 reps of *Bs dec* (6 sts)
- Bring it to a close. Finish filling the head and sew up the hole with the tail, then weave in the ends.

Pattern of Ears using cream or black yarn

- R1: Ch 5, inc 1 sc 3, ch 5, inc 1 sc 3
- Finish with a long tail to stitch with. Weave the tail neatly down to the ear's bottom corner. Stitch the ears to the head on R14 using the same tail.

Pattern of Body using white or cream yarn

- The berry stitch is also used on the body.

- R1: Ch 2, 6 sc in the 2nd ch from hook; R2: Ch 2, 6 sc into 2nd ch from hook; R3: Ch 2,

- Rep R2: *sc in the next st, bs in the same st as the last sc* 6 times more (12 sts)

- R3: *Sc 1, 1 bs and 1 sc in the next st, bs 1, 1 sc & 1 bs in the next st, bs 1, 1 sc and 1 bs in the next st* repeat 3 times (18 sts)

- Rep R4: *sc 1,1 sc bs 1, and 1 bs in next st* 6 times more (24 sts)

- R5: 12 reps of *Bs 1, sc 1* (24 sts)

- R6: 12 reps of *sc 1, BS 1* (24 sts)

- R7-10: Rep R5-6 4 more times for a total of four rounds (24 stitches).

- Finish with a long tail to stitch with. Stuff it tightly and stitch it to the head with the long tail that has been created and the tapestry needle over around R8-15 of the head.

Pattern of feet from the black yarn

- R1: ch 2, 5 sc into 2nd ch at hook; R2: Ch 2, 5 sc into 2nd ch on hook; R3: Ch 2

- Switch to cream yarn if knitting a white and cream lamb; otherwise, continue in black.

- Sc throughout all 5 Sts (2 circles total – 5 Sts) R2-3: Sc throughout all 5 sts

- Finish with a long tail to stitch with. Stitch the two rear feet to the body's R8-10 and the bottom two feet to the body's R4-7.

Pattern of tail using white or cream yarn

- Ch 4, beginning in the 2nd ch from the hook, bs 1, sc 1, and then bs 1

- Finish with a long tail to stitch with. Sew the underside of the body together and weave in all the loose ends.

- And that's it.

4.5 Baby Blanket Crochet Pattern

You want a quick and easy blanket when you first start how to crochet so you will not have to wait weeks to see the outcomes of your efforts. When it comes to crochet baby blankets, this one is a quick and simple job. Chain stitch and single crochet are the only crochet stitches used. Additionally, using a bigger hook size gives the blanket more drape and speeds up the process.

This design is simple enough for beginners, but it's also suitable for crocheter of any and all skill levels looking for a quick and simple project. This crochet pattern is great for contemplative crochet because it has a simple repetition and just requires basic crochet stitches. It's the kind of quick crochet baby blanket you can make while sitting in the vehicle, waiting in lines, or watching TV.

Equipment / Tools

Tapestry needle

Crochet hook

Stitch marker

Materials

Baby yarn

Size

The preemie, infant, and toddler sizes are all included in this crochet baby blanket pattern. The lowest size is listed first, with modifications for bigger sizes mentioned in parenthesis.

If you choose to add a baby blanket border, your completed blanket would be a little bit larger than the proportions below.

The smallest blanket is roughly 26 inches broad and 34 inches length for preemies. If you want to crochet the blanket using Bernat Softee yarn, you'll need two to three (5-oz) skeins of yarn, based on how tight you crochet. You'll need around 724 yards/662 meters for the blanket design, plus a little more for the gauge swatch, in terms of yardage.

The mid-sized newborn/receiving blanket is around 30 inches square. If you like a blanket with a more rectangular form, you may make it a little longer. If so, strive for a size of 30" x 34." Based on how tightly you crochet, you'll need two to three 5-oz Bernat Softee balls for this size.

Toddler: The blanket measured 36 inches by 44 inches is the largest of the bunch. To crochet this size, you'll need four 5-oz Bernat Softee balls.

Gauge

When crocheting the pattern as explained below, 4 stitches = 1 inch.

Row gauge: For this design, row gauge is unimportant.

Pattern and Instructions

- Ch 105 (121, 145). Please keep in mind that these instructions are for the preemie or the small size with the medium and larger size in parenthesis.

- In the first ch from the hook, place a stitch marker. Sc in the third ch from the hook [Skip next ch and sc in the next ch.] Repeat for the rest of the row. Turn the first ch.

- [sc in the first sp of the following ch-1 row, ch 1.] Repeat the bracketed sequence for the remaining row. Stitch a sc st further into st where you inserted the marker at the end of the row; you can withdraw the marker prior working the stitch. Turn the first ch.

- The remaining rows are identical to row 2, with one small exception: at the end of a row, work your final sc st into the previous row's turning chain. Repeat this row till the baby blanket is the length you want it to be.

- Cut the yarn once the baby blanket reaches the desired length, leaving around six inches of excess yarn. Thread the yarn end onto the tapestry needle and weave the loose thread of the yarn to the blanket using the needle. Continue with any additional loose ends dangling from the blanket.

- This crochet design is good without any extra edging, but if you want to, you may add one. You may select from a variety of baby blanket edgings. A basic single crochet stitch across the blanket's whole edge is a simple choice that complements the single crochet motif in this pattern.

4.6 Crochet Mitten Pattern

There's nothing quite like putting on a pair of handcrafted mittens in your favorite yarn colour and venturing out into the cold. The cuffs made of puff stich will tight exactly around the wrists for a wonderful fit in this glove pattern, which was created to keep you warm and comfy. This Mitten pattern is a fantastic pattern choice whether you're making a pair of these lovely mittens for yourself or crafting pieces to keep family and friends warm.

Size

Small: 9.5 inches in length x 4 in width (fingers) (24 x 10 cm)

Large: 10.5 inches in length x 4.5 in width (fingers) (26.5 x 11 cm)

Tools/ Equipment

Crochet hook size I/9 (5.5 mm) for small size

Crochet hook size J/10 (6.0 mm) for large size

Ring stitch marker

Tapestry needle

Materials

Approximately 85 yards aran or worsted weight yarn per mitten (small), 100 yards aran or worsted weight yarn (large).

Gauge

13 stitches & 16 rows in single crochet using size I hook = 4 inches

12 stitches & 15 rows in single crochet using size J hook = 4 inches

Special Stitches

Puff Stitch/ Bean Stitch

*yarn over and insert the hook in the same stitch, pull down, repeat from * 2 additional times, yarn over; pull across 8 loops on the hook, ch 1 (to lock stitch). Following the bean stitch, skip 1 stitch. In the design, this will yield two stitches.

2 Stitches Together in Single Crochet

Insert the hook into the stitch, yarn over (yo) and pull across stitch (2 stitches on the hook), yarn over (yo) and pull across stitch (3 stitches on the hook), yarn over again and pull through all three stitches on hook.

Pattern and Instructions

- For teen/adult tiny mittens, use hook size I/9 (5.5mm).
- For adult sizes medium/large, use hook size J/10 (6.0 mm).
- (Make two because the pattern is the same for left and right hands.)
- To connect, chain 3 and slip stitch.
- 1st round: Each stitch of the beginning chain has two single crochet loops. Total stitches: 6
- Second round: *Single crochet into the back loop of the first stitch of the round, single crochet into the front loop of the first stitch of the round, repeat from * for the rest of the round. (12)
- Place a stitch marker or start marking rounds with a piece of yarn. For each cycle forward, move the marker up or weave the thread up.
- 3rd round: *Single crochet into the back loop of the first stitch of the round, single crochet into the front loop of the

first stitch of the round, repeat from * for the rest of the round (24)

- 4th round: *Single crochet into the back loop of the first stitch of round, and now single crochet into the front loop of the first stitch of round, repetition in next stitch, omit 1 stitch, **single crochet to the back loop of the next stitch, single crochet the front loop of the same stitch, skip 1 stitch, replicate from ** once more, single crochet into the back loop of the next stitch, single crochet for front loop of the same stitch, skip 1 stitch, reiterate from ** once more, single crochet into the back loop of the next stitch, single crochet for front loop of the same stitch, repeat from (30)

- Rounds 5 to 20: *Single crochet into the back loop of the first stitch of the round, single crochet into the front loop of the first stitch of the round, miss 1 stitch, continue from * for the rest of the round. (30)

- Round 21: Skip 3 stitches, *single crochet through back loop of the next stitch of round, single crochet for front loop of next stitch of round, weakly chain 7 stitches (create thumb hole), miss 3 stitches, *single crochet through back loop of next stitch of the round, single crochet for front loop of the next stitch of round, miss 1 stitch, repeat from * for remaining portion of round (35)

- Round 22: 4 basic single crochet, 2 stitches of single crochet together, *single crochet to back loop of the next stitch of the round, single crochet for front loop of the same stitch, miss 1 stitch, replicate from * for rest of round (34)

- Round 23: 2 stitches of single crochet together, 3 basic single crochet, 2 stitches of single crochet together twice, *single crochet in and out of back loop of the next stitch of round, sc into front loop of the same stitch, miss 1 stitch, rehearse from * for rest of round (32)

- Round 24: 1 basic single crochet, 2 stitches of single crochet together, 1 basic single crochet, 2 stitches of single crochet together, *single crochet in and out of back loop of the next stitch of round, sc* crochet for front loop of the same stitch, miss 1 stitch, rehearse from * for rest of round. (30)

- Round 25: *Single crochet in and out to back loop of the next stitch of round, sc* into the front loop of the same stitch, 2 stitches of single crochet together 2 times, miss 1 stitch, repeating from * for rest of round. (28)

- Round 26: *sc into the back loop of this next stitch of the round, sc into front loop of the same stitch, 2 stitches of single crochet together twice, miss 1 stitch, resume from * for remaining of round. (26)

- Round 27: *sc into the back loop of this next stitch from round, sc into front loop of the same stitch, 2 stitches together single crochet 2 times, skip 1 stitch, repeating from * for rest of round. (24)

- Rounds 28 – 29: *Single crochet in and out of back loop of the first stitch of round, sc into front loop of the first stitch of round, miss 1 stitch, replicate from * to last 2 stitches of the round, slip stitch into rear loop of second to the last stitch of the round, slip stitch for front loop of second to the last stitch of round, miss last stitch of round, replicate from * for last 2 stitches of the round, slip stitch into rear loop of second to the last stitch of the round, slip stitch for front loop of second to the last stitch of round, miss last stitch of round, (24)

- Round 30: Slip stitch loosely in each stitch of the circle (24)

- Round 31: Bean stitch all the way around the row. (12 beans = 2 stitches per bean)

- Round 32: *Single crochet into the back loop of the first stitch of the round, single crochet into the front loop of the first stitch of the round, miss 1 stitch, bean stitch, continue from * for the rest of the round. (24)

- Round 33: Bean stitch all the way around the row (12 beans)

- Round 34: *Single crochet into the back loop of the first stitch of the round, single crochet into the front loop of the first stitch of the round, miss 1 stitch, bean stitch, continue from * for the rest of the round. (24)

- Round 35: Bean stitch all the way around the row (12 beans)
- Round 36: Slip stitch loosely in each stitch of the circle (24)
- Fasten off and weave the ends in.

Thumb

- Slip stitches the yarn to the thumb hole where the thumb and finger meet; this is not counted as a stitch. (Thumb is done in a spiral pattern.)
- Round 1: 14 single crochet stitches (14)
- Round 2: 2 single crochets joined together, total of 12 single crochets. (13)
- Round 3: There are thirteen single crochet stitches (13)
- Round 4: 2 single crochets, 2 single crochets together, 11 single crochets (12)
- Round 5: 10 single crochet, 2 single crochet, 2 single crochet, 2 single crochet, 2 single crochet, 2 single crochet, 2 (11)
- Round 6: There are eleven single crochet stitches (11)
- Round 7: 2 together Single crochets, 9 single crochet. (10)
- Round 8: *Single crochet 2 stiches together, repeat from * around for the rest of the round. (5)

Finishing:

- Toggle the mitten to the wrong side. Weave the ends in. To finish, turn the thumb to the wrong side and thread yarn through the top of the thumb hole.
- Return the mitten to the right side.

4.7 Crochet Pattern For Autumn Sweater

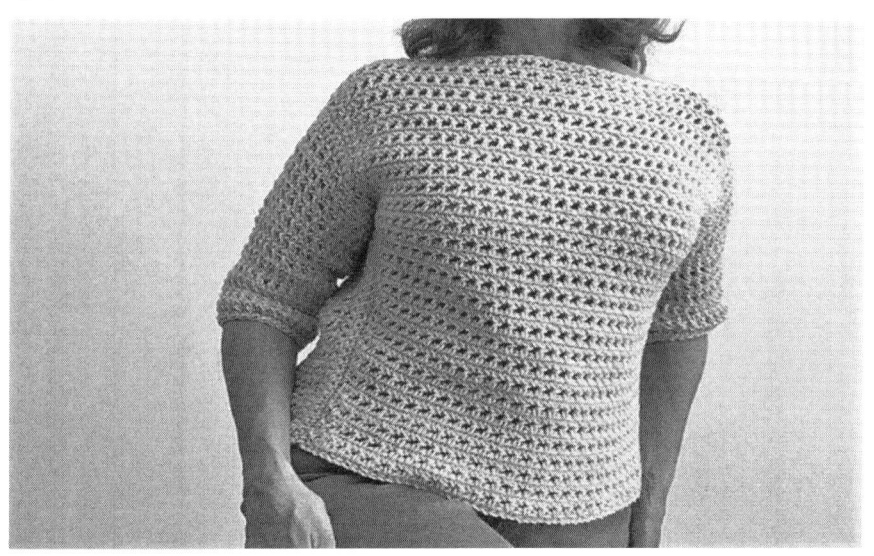

Here is a simple crochet design for an autumn sweater. This 3/4-sleeved top is ideal for transitioning from summer to fall. You can make it in the season's most popular colour: Warm Blush.

Of course, it's a great spring sweater as well. Warm Blush is a lovely, soft colour that would be ideal for spring. So simple, There is no difference between the front and rear panels, and there is no rising or decreasing! It's ideal for beginners.

Dimensions

19.5 inches long from shoulder to bottom for size small. At the waist, it's 16 inches wide.

The cotton yarn used in this has a lot of drape and elasticity to it.

Materials

Cotton yarn: (3.5 skeins) or 12.25 oz.

Size H of crochet hook

Gauge

3 hdc = 1 inches, 3 rows (2 hdc + 1 sc)= 1 inches.

Pattern and Instructions

- Ch 67

- Row 1: single crochet in 2nd ch from the hook, *ch 1, sk 1 ch, sc in the next ch*; row 2: single crochet in 2nd ch from the hook, *ch 1, sk 1 ch, sc in next ch*; row 3: sc into the last three ch's, repetition from * to *. Ch 1, sc in ea of the last two ch's. Ch 2. Turn

- Row 2: hdc in centre of 1st sc beneath, *ch 1, hdc in centre of next sc*. Repetition from * to * to the last sc. Ch 1, sk to the last sc, hdc in turning ch. Ch 1. Turn

- Row 3: Sc in the first sp below, *ch 1, sc in the next sp*. Repetition from * to * to the last sp. Do not ch, sc in the last sp, *sc in the turning ch. Ch 2. Turn

- Rows 2 and 3 should be repeated for a total number of 55 rows (27 hdc rows), finishing with a sc row.

- 2 rows of scs should be uniformly spaced along either side of the panel. Approximately 52 sc

- Attach the panels

- Bring the correct sides of the panels together. Attach at the shoulders with a yarn needle and slip stitch for about 4" from the edge, moving toward the centre.

- Attach with yarn needle at sides, stopping 9" below shoulder, and sl sts to bottom.

Sleeves

- Put hook at the hole of sleeve bottom opening at seam, working right side out.

- Row 1: connect yarn with a sl st, sc together in the same st, hdc in the next sp, ea sp around. To connect the start sc, sl st.

- Row 2: ch 1, sc in first st, *ch 1, sk 1, sc in the next st, ch 1* To finish, repeat pattern from * to *. To join, stitch sl.

- Row 3: ch 2, hdc in the start of 1st sc, *ch 1, hdc in top of next sc, ch 1*; row 4: ch 2, hdc in the start of 1st sc, *ch 1, hdc in top of next sc, ch 1*; row 5: ch 2, to finish, repeat the pattern from * to *. To join, type sl.

- Row 4: ch 1, sc in the first sp, sc in the top of 1st hdc, *sc in the next sp, to finish, repeat the pattern from * to *. To join, use sl.
- Row 5: ch 2, hdc in centre of the 1st sc, ch 1, sk 1, hdc in the center of next sc, ch 1, sk 1, hdc in mid of next sc, ch 1, sk 1. Ch 1, and repeat until the last sc.
- Row 6: ch1, 1 sc in first sp, *ch 1, 1 sc in the next sp, ch1* To finish, repeat the pattern from * to *. Join.
- Row 7: ch 2, 1st sc hdc, *ch 1, 1st sc hdc, ch 1* To finish, repeat the pattern from * to *. Join.
- Row 8 is the same as Row 6.
- Row 9 is the same as Row 7.
- Row 10: Row 6 is repeated.
- Row 11: Row 7 is repeated.
- Row 12: Row 6 is repeated.
- Row 13: ch 2 and hdc in each stitch (no ch's between stitches)
- Row 14: ch 1, *sc in each stitch (no ch's between stitches)
- Row 15: ch 2, 1st sc hdc, *ch 1, 1st sc hdc, ch 1* To finish, repeat the pattern from * to *. Join.

- Row 16: ch 1, sc in each st until the end (no ch's between rows). Join

- Row 17: ch 2, 1st sc hdc, *ch 1, 1st sc hdc, ch 1* To finish, repeat the pattern from * to *. Join.

- Row 18: ch 1and sc in each stitch (no ch's between stitches) Join

- Rows 19–24 are the same as rows 17 and 18.

- Row 25: ch 2 and hdc in each stitch (no ch's between stitches) Join

- Row 26: ch 1, *sc in each stitch (no ch's between stitches). Finish it off.

- Repeat for the second sleeve.

Chapter 5: What Every Beginner Crocheter Should Know?

5.1 With A Pattern Repetition, How Do You Change Your Base Chain?

After realizing that while the majority of the blankets patterns are baby blanket size, you may wish to make the blanket larger at times. There is 'pattern repeat' at the start of most of the patterns so that you may change the pattern to any size you like. It is also attempted to do this with a lot of the scarf and cap patterns, so you may tailor them to the person for whom you're making them.

When it is stated that the pattern repeats any multiple of ten plus one, it means that you must multiply any number by ten (for example, 9 x 10) and then add one (so the base chain will be 91.)

Working out a practice swatch of the design you're creating with the yarn you've selected and measuring it to determine your base chain is the easiest method to make the blanket the size you desire.

If the pattern repetition is a multiple of 10 plus 1, for example, you might construct a base chain of 21 and then work just few rows of the pattern. Assume you've measured the swatch and its 5 inches wide, and then your completed blanket will be 40 inches in width. 40 inches when divided by 5 inches equals to 8, so multiply 21 by 8 to obtain a 168-inch base chain. Because 168 isn't a valid number for the pattern repetition, you need to round it up to 171, which again are 17 x 10, plus 1.

The same approach applies to designs in which there is no pattern repetition and you may chain any number to construct the blanket - simply knit out a tiny sample and measure it to get your base chain.

5.2 Which Chain Should You Start With?

You'll flip your work and continue working back down the chain to construct the first row once you've settled in with your base chain. Most of the designs instruct you to begin by hooking onto the second, third, or fourth chain from the hook.

5.3 The Question Of How Much Yarn To Purchase?

If you're making a blanket that's exactly the same size as one of the patterns, you can usually buy the suggested amount of yarn in the pattern and be OK, but it is always recommended saving the receipts instance you have extras you want to return. Some individuals use more yarns than others because everyone crochets distinctively and with a different tension.

Unfortunately, no one can suggest you a precise amount of yarn if you're altering a pattern to a new size that haven't been created previously. Designers often have to predict how much yarn a blanket will require when creating it for the first time, and sometimes they have extras and sometimes they need to purchase more.

You can, however, make some educated guesses. If you wish to almost double size of a pattern for a 30 x 40-inch baby blanket, for example, simply twice the quantity of yarn the pattern requires for and you'll likely have enough yarn. It's always a great idea to maintain receipts.

5.4 How To Alter The Colors?

Stop just before your last stitch to change colors at the end of a row, drop the color you've been working with, and draw a loop through the new color.

For example, if you're working on a row of single crochet stich, you'd enter your hook, yarn over, and draw up a loop on the final stitch, then pause with two loops on your hook. Drop the yarn you've been using and pull your new color through the two loops. Once you pull through with using the new color, leave approximately a six-inch tail, then snip off the old color, leaving another six-inch tail to weave into the blanket later.

Then you simply follow the pattern after pulling through with the new colour, so for a row of stich of single crochet, you will chain one with new colour and turn.

If you're using a stitch apart from single crochet to change colours, just pull through using a new colour exactly before the stitch is finished. So, if you were crocheting a puff stitch having many loops on the hook, you will draw through all the loops with the different colour just before you were completing the puff.

5.5 How To Secure The Ends And Weave Them In?

When the instructions say to tie off after you've completed all of the rows of the crochet creation, this means you should take the loop on your hook and draw it up until it's 6 to 9 inches long. The loop should then be terminated right at the top: Then you'll pull the yarn that's still tied to the yarn ball away from the yarn ball and tighten the tail that's linked to the blanket until it forms a knot. Then, using a big tapestry needle, weave that last tail, as well as any additional tails you might have from the start of the blanket or even from changing colours, into the blanket.

5.6 What Is The Best Way To Block A Blanket?

When the tension is a little inconsistent after finishing a blanket, or the border has to be straightened out a little, you should block the blankets by getting them damp and pinning them as straight and flat as you can. Best way is to generally wet the blanket with a spray bottle loaded with water, then dry it on foam board and pin the borders to keep them straight. You may also wash the blanket per the label's instructions before laying it out to dry on a foam board.

5.7 How Do You Frog?

The final, but certainly not least, essential skill for every beginner crocheter is the ability to frog. If you make a mistake, frogging simply means redoing your crochet work and beginning again. This is something we have to do almost every time we produce a blanket.

The easiest approach to improve your crochet skills is to double-check your work after a few rows and correct any errors as early as you see them. Even if it hurts, it will improve your crocheting skills and help you feel more pleased of your completed product.

However, if you make an error that you don't see until the very end, understand that there are no crochet cops, and even the most crooked objects may be lovely. There's plenty more yarn out there for you to experiment with.

Chapter 6: 10 Common Mistakes and How to Prevent Them?

It's difficult to keep track of everything when you first begin crocheting as there are many new words and methods to master. You could feel as if you're drowning in all you need to know about crochet patterns, gauge, keeping your project straight, and so many more. Some Individuals had such a difficult time learning what needed to know as a beginner crocheter. They kept making mistakes and couldn't figure out how to correct them. That's why if you're a beginner crocheter, this will walk you through 10 of the most frequent beginner crochet mistakes and how to prevent them.

6.1 Not Being Able To Distinguish Between Chains

One of the basic stitches you learn while starting to crochet is chain stitches that are the basic stitches of any crochet creation. In a crochet design, the first round or row will usually instruct you to begin crocheting in the next chain from the hook, and then continue crocheting in the remaining chains in the row. Furthermore, all of the loops begin to resemble one another, and how can you determine which is which?

You'll have a string of chain stitches after completing the number of chains specified in the design. The first chain is the loop on your hook right now, and the next chain is the loop afterwards. It may appear that the portion at the end of the loop on the hook is the second chain, and you want to proceed to the second loop, which is the hook's second chain. Then, as you work your way down the string of chain stitches, make a stitch in each of the loops until you reach the end.

When it's difficult to see which stitches are which, put the work flat on a table and smooth everything out until it's all matched up. Then you'll be able to see what the chain that you just crocheted in looks like and know what the next stitch is.

6.2 Maintaining Order In Your Project

One of the most difficult aspects of crocheting when you're just starting out is keeping the project straight while you're working on a flat item. When initially taught, people sometimes convert a square wash cloth into a horseshoe shape. Now, the project may not be as badly misplaced, but it's not uncommon for a component with straight edges to start looking curved. This issue has a straightforward fix.

If the project begins to curve in all the incorrect ways, it's most likely because you added stitches where they weren't needed. This might happen if you add two stitches to one of stitches in the row although you don't need to increase, causing the row to alter form. Or, more commonly, the very last stitch of the row is done in the incorrect stitch. When you get to the end of a row, make sure your last stitch is crocheted on top of the very first stitch from previous row. You don't want to stitch through the chains that began that round. If you sew the last stitch there, you'll end up with one additional stitch than you should have, causing your flat piece to curve.

If you're having trouble determining where the top of last stitch of the row is, look at the two loops on head of the stitch. Keep a record of them. Rather than the usual post that perhaps a crochet stitch has and the two loops at the apex which you had put the hook through, the chains will have one loop and a strand. Your product will stay straight the entire time if you keep records of placement of the stiches.

6.3 Not Understanding Gauge

Gauge is an aspect of crocheting that is sometimes overlooked because it is not well understood or because individuals just do not want to cope with it. If you had been crocheting and had entirely neglected to keep track of the gauge, which meant that your creations didn't fit. So, what exactly is gauge, and why do we require it? The number of stitches as well as rows you can fit on a 4" × 4" square termed as a gauge swatch is referred to as gauge. Certain stitch numbers are critical for garment size. Designers would be unable to measure clothes without a gauge swatch, and garments would arrive in a variety of sizes. Even if you're not a designer, you might be wondering why you'd need to produce a gauge swatch. Gauge swatches, on the other hand, are just as important for the crocheter as they are for the designer. If your gauge does not match what the pattern specifies for while sewing a garment or other item, the finished product will be an entirely different size. That means if you're sewing size medium clothing and the swatch has a little more stitches than that of the swatch specifies, your finished product will be smaller in size than the medium size you expected. Your product will be larger than a medium if you use fewer stitches than the gauge asks for.

How can you know whether your gauges are correct? Prepare a 4"x 4" square well with required number of stitches and rows according to the gauge. You're good to go if it matches. If you have extra stitches than the pattern asks for, your tension is tighter, therefore move up a hook size to crochet the stitches bigger. If you have fewer stitches, your stitches are too large, and you'll need to move down a hook size to get the right quantity in. Once you've found the appropriate gauge, you're ready to begin your crochet creation. Make sure you devote enough time to this stage; if you neglected it for far too long, then your crocheting will be deteriorated as a result. Yes, it will take a bit longer to get started, but will not be disappointed.

6.4 Weaving In The Ends Correctly

You'll see strands of yarn poking out of your craft that you don't want to show up when it's finished. Weaving them in is a good way to remedy them. One of the most difficult aspects of crochet is weaving in ends. It's not that it's difficult; it's simply that it's not enjoyable. However, if the weaving in of ends isn't done correctly, it might cause problems. You don't want to merely cut them off since it will cause your project to unwind too easily. Instead, leave a lengthy end to weave in as you're trimming. You'll start weaving after threading a yarn needle with strand of yarn. You'll be threading it all through different threads as you weave in the finish, but don't do it in a straight line. Instead, begin weaving in one way and then switch to the other. This will cause the woven in to bend, making it more difficult to remove. Whip stitch can also be used to weave the ends in and prevent them from popping out. After you've woven it in as much as you can, snip off the remaining end as near as you can.

6.5 Difficulty In Joining Rounds Correctly

When you're working on a circular project, you'll often see a term that reads "join the circle." This may be very difficult for beginners because it isn't how you normally go onto the next row while working a flat design. When a beginner initially starts crocheting, they had no idea how to connect in the round. They always start the round on the wrong stitch and ended it on the wrong thread as well. This mess up the stitch count, which threw the remainder of the design off. But that is something that anyone can be easily remedied.

Let's start by going through how to connect a line of chain stitches to start the project in the round. After you've completed the strand of chain stitches, link the initial chain with a slip stitch at the end of the row to construct your item in the round. When you link the strands of chains, it's possible for them to get tangled, which will make the underside of your product appear different than you desire. To avoid this, lay the chain stitches outwards in a circle, as if you're about to connect them, and check to see whether they're twisted. If the strand of chain stiches is twisted, untwist it and connect the strands together to form a circle once it looks good.

If you're crocheting in the round, you'll be connecting it if it's not done in continuous rounds. The row (or round) will begin with one or two chains (depending on the stitch) at the first stitch that will form the section that you'll connect at the start of the round. It's essentially a stitch marker. After that, crochet in each stitch all the way to the finish of the circle. When you come to the end of the circle, be careful not to work a stitch into the chain 2 stitches. As a result, the round has an excessive number of stitches. Pause at the stitch before the first, and afterwards slip stitch to the second of the two chains you formed to complete the circle. This completes the round and makes it a complete row. It can take a little while to get used to this, but you'll be fine in no time.

6.6 Not Knowing How To Read Crochet Patterns Correctly

Crochet patterns appear to be a totally new language when you just start crocheting. You see many of the abbreviations you'll need to know, and they all look like crazy to you. But don't worry; after you read more patterns, you'll be capable of reading them as if you were born with them. Design notes, supplies, abbreviations used, gauge, and the pattern itself are all split down into the same exact elements in crochet patterns. The hook size, yarn, and other materials you'll need to complete the design will be listed in the supply list. If you want your creation to be of the same size as the design, use the same yarn weight and hook size as the pattern specifies. The abbreviations list will show you which stitches are used in the patterns and what acronyms are used to represent them. Most crochet stitches are segmented into abbreviations to make the design easier to understand and to keep the pattern length to a minimum. To make it easier to understand what they're saying, the abbreviations are nearly always the same. The pattern notes part will inform you of any additional information you should be aware of before beginning to crochet the design. In a 4" by 4" square, the gauge portion will indicate you how much stitches and rows you will obtain. For further information, see the gauge section above. After that, you'll come to the pattern itself, which has all of the directions for creating it.

6.7 Not Understanding The Pattern In Its Entirety

Beginner crocheter sometimes leap into a project that appears to be fun, without first reading the instructions, only to discover they have no clue how to complete it. You should always go through a crochet pattern completely before beginning it. You'll be able to determine whether there are any stitches or techniques you'll need to master as you go through the pattern. Frequently, patterns will include instructions in areas that are beyond the abilities of a beginner. Crochet patterns generally include lessons on how to attach garments or components to a crochet project, as well as links to pattern or stitch instructions for unique stitches that some may not be familiar with. You'll be able to see most of these by reading the pattern, ensuring that you won't have to stop crocheting midway through to learn a different technique. Even if you wait until later in the pattern to learn it, reading the pattern will alert you there is something new to discover. It might also give you a good idea if you want to create the design now or wait until later.

6.8 Not Using Stich Markers For Marking Start Of Round

Stitch markers are especially useful if you're working on a pattern with a complex stitch pattern which has repetitions. You can use a marker to mark the beginning of each repeat so you don't miss one while crocheting. When dealing with lace designs, this is very useful. The stitch markers you use don't have to be certified stitch markers. You can u use yarn strands or indeed a piece of paper if don't have any on hand. Stitch markers are always a nice thing to have on hand, no matter what you're doing.

6.9 Not Grasping The Concept Of Tension

As you complete additional patterns, you'll notice that the term "tension" is frequently used. And what does it mean in the context of crochet? The tightness of your sutures is referred to as tension. If your tension is tight, the cloth you're making with your yarn will be tight, with very little openness in the stitches. When you have a slack tension, your stitches will be open and loose. The objective is to maintain consistent tension across the project, so that the stitch tightness does not change as you work. Your stitches may be tighter while crocheting since you are tugging on the yarn further as you complete a stitch, which tightens it. Alternatively, you may not be tugging the yarn tight enough, resulting in larger stitches. To prevent moving too far one way or another, tug on the stitch just enough to make it loose, but not too tight.

6.10 Using The Wrong Hook Size And Yarn For The Task

When you first begin crocheting and have never worked with fibre arts before, hook sizes and yarn may appear to be the same. Isn't it simply yarn and a hook? When you start looking at designs, you'll see terms like yarn weight and 6mm hook being used. You might be wondering, "What's the big deal about these?" and "Why do they matter?" Well, the yarn and hook size used in the project will affect the size of your item as well as the quality of your stitches. If you are using a weight 5 yarn instead of a weight 3 yarn for a project that asks for a thin yarn, your creation will be much larger than you anticipated. So, whether you're sewing clothing or even a stuffed animal, your finished product will be much larger than the pattern specifies. The hook size is the same way. The stitches will be larger if the hook size is larger. In most designs, multiple hook sizes are required for different yarn weights. If you really want the stitches to be quite tight and tiny, use a small hook size; if you want bigger stitches, choose a larger hook size. So, if a project specifies a specific hook size and yarn weight, be sure you use it if you want the product to turn out exactly the size it specifies.

Conclusion

Crocheting is beneficial to both the mind and the emotions. After learning three or four fundamental crochet stitches, the crocheter can use them to create objects that are made up of numerous repeats of the same stitch in a contemplative manner. Some of the crocheters use this craft as a kind of meditation, while others use it as a form of prayer. Many crocheters will tell you that crocheting helps to relieve stress and lightens a depressed soul.

Crocheting for oneself allows you to make lovely items to wear or place around your home to brighten your mood. Crochet may be donated to charities, giving you a feeling of purpose and compassion.

Crocheting is beneficial to the mind since each design requires the formation of new brain synapses or connections. Learning to interpret patterns or diagrams trains the brain in entirely new ways, keeping one nimble. Try your hand at crocheting…It takes some time to get over the learning hump, but once you have learned, it'll be well worth it.

Printed in Great Britain
by Amazon